Pickpocket Poetica

Also by Scott Keeney

Early Returns

Sappho Does Hay(na)ku

Walloping Shrug

Pickpocket Poetica

Scott Keeney

SOME CLOUDS PRESS

Copyright © 2018 Scott Keeney

Book design by Scott Keeney
Cover photo by Christine Mulia
Typeset in Dante MT

ISBN 978-1-948728-92-8 (paperback)
ISBN 978-1-948728-93-5 (ebook)

PUBLICATION HISTORY

First ebook edition: June 2007
Revised and expanded print edition: September 2018

CONTENTS

Acknowledgments ix

The Individual Talent 1

Timepiece 2

Three After (Niedecker) 3

Shadowgraph 4

Word Problem 5

Thought 6

After Otomo No Yakamochi (718–785) 7

Carbon Copy 8

Aubade 9

A Relationship 10

My Love Has Little Mercy 11

After Ted Berrigan 12

Loveless 13

Rough Trade 14

Epiphany 15

Custodian 16

Resolve 17

Man-Child 18

Loveless 19

Pulp 20

Strike 21

Dad 22

Moving 23

Night 24

The Pulley—or, Thirteen Ways
to Rock-n-Roll with a Blackbird 25

History 29

Capital 30

Memorandum 31

A Reading Public 32

Death 33

Confessional 34

Loveless 35

Rimbaud Considers the Future 36

Poem 37

Eventriloquist 38

Sleep 39

Edgar 40

Native Piece 41

Poem 42

Loveless 43

Grain 44

Now 45

Retrofuturism 46

Transformative Limitation 47

Scintilla 48

Morning 49

Populism, Criticism, Art 50

Some Lonesome   51

Autumn   54

Sight   55

Affectionate   56

Rain (after Creeley)   57

Query   58

A Stop & Shop in Connecticut   59

Faith   60

Morning   61

Pain Song, A Cento   62

Good God   63

Fling   64

In Time, Dear   65

To and Fro   66

Fixing the Reception   67

If We Could Take the Long, Long View, Patriarchy Might Be Seen as Ephemeral, or At Least We Can Hope   68

Paper Cuts   69

An Escamoteur of Aesthetics   70

The Sun after Kerouac   73

An Elegy for Ginsberg   74

Sunday Morning   75

Praxis   76

Another Piece   77

Joe Mo   78

Oppen Ended   79

Game   80

Cringe   81

Bio Note   82

Sic   83

Advice   84

Speech   85

Sing! Sing!   86

Guest   87

Bodhisattva Blues   88

Opening   89

Song   90

Frank Sinatra   91

Small Talk   92

Grit   93

American Seasonals   94

Garde Down   96

Helpless   97

Riddle   98

Petty Lament   99

Untitled (White and Black)   100

Death   101

Collision   102

An Evening   103

Echo   104

Finale   105

The Weatherman   106

ACKNOWLEDGMENTS

My thanks to the editors of the publications in which the following poems first appeared, sometimes in different versions or under different titles.

Blackbird 2: "The Pulley—or, Thirteen Ways to Rock-n-Roll with a Blackbird"

Columbia Poetry Review: "After Otomo No Yakamochi (718-785)"; "After Ted Berrigan"; "The Individual Talent"; "My Love Has Little Mercy"; "A Relationship"; "Sic"; "To and Fro"; and "Word Problem" (all originally published as "from Pickpocket Poetica")

Court Green: "Death" and "Three After (Niedecker)"

gestalten: "Bio Note"; "Edgar"; and "A body without time" and "Mainly my cup of coffee" from "An Escamoteur of Aesthetics" (all originally published without titles as "from The Escamoteur of Aesthetics")

The Hay(na)ku Anthology, Volume II: "A Stop & Shop in Connecticut" and "The Weatherman"

Lilliput Review: "Confessional"; "Fixing the Reception"; and "Dirty dishes in the sink" from "An Escamoteur of Aesthetics" (originally published as "The End Review")

The New Verse News: "Cringe"

No Fresh Cut Flowers: "Collision"

Noon: Journal of the Short Poem: "Now" and "Query"

Otoliths: "Untitled (White and Black)"

Peaky Hide: "Custodian"; "Resolve"; "Man-Child"; and "Pulp" (all originally published without titles as "from The Escamoteur of Aesthetics")

Ribot: "History"; "Loveless ('The sky, when it')"; "Loveless ('Going around my place')"; "Moving"; and "Thought" (all originally published without titles as "from The Escamoteur of Aesthetics")

ugly duckling: "Poem (Inside the piece of paper)"; "Retrofuturism"; "Rimbaud Considers the Future"; "Transformative Limitation"; and the following pieces from "An Escamoteur of Aesthetics": "Tabletalk. Crosswalk."; "I play the sugar drums and relegate"; "The triangle goes Poof!"; "The myth of the right poetics"; "Big tree."; "It's raining cats and dogs."; and "Well then" (all originally published without titles as "from The Escamoteur of Aesthetics")

Whiskey Island Magazine: "Sight"

As for wanting to find . . . a broader & loftier meaning to take home after the performance, together with the program and ice-cream stick, I cannot see the point in doing so.

SAMUEL BECKETT

Pickpocket Poetica

THE INDIVIDUAL TALENT

So as not to wear my feelings on my sleeve,
I slipped into my objective correlative shoes.
They suitably contained all that I felt or believed,
But inside I was singing the hollow man blues.

TIMEPIECE

The problem
with clocks
these days,
so few
have faces
to save.

THREE AFTER (NIEDECKER)

SUNDAY AGAIN

Green shards
of sun blink
on the front walk

as the wet dawn
gives way to the dry
island of day

AGAINST THE WORLD

Thumb burn
   of the waffle
      iron—my love:

Soothing cold
   bottle of
      pure maple syrup

NIGHT AGAIN

Twilight wraps
the white feline
neck of day

lands on the bare
body of water
blue silk scarf

you never wear
but oh well
the night will

SHADOWGRAPH

after Ed Sanders and *Plato*

Poets live with
one foot in
the Grail and
the other, fuck
if I know.

WORD PROBLEM

for Ron Padgett

1. None of us really knows what to write
   as we watch the pus gathering around heaven
   sores opening where clouds once were,
   but the thing is we are given
2. A kind of lukewarm craziness of heart.

THOUGHT

It's hard
to imagine
a better
obsession.

AFTER OTOMO NO YAKAMOCHI (718–785)

Law and Order over,
I turn off the light and wait
for sleep's fur-lined cuffs.

CARBON COPY

At night, when our bodies lie
next to each other, asleep,
they unfold themselves
like small dark buds,
making the same shape,
belying what secrets we keep.

AUBADE

all across in
morning's fields
water leaves
little shoes

in morning's beds
bodies touch
like envelopes
and pens in desks

A RELATIONSHIP

Bing! goes the microwave.

"Your coffee's done."

"It's not coffee. It's carrots."

MY LOVE HAS LITTLE MERCY

When I make myself her horse
it feels like a blind curve
I want to lay myself to rest
in the surface of the Brass River
carve her name upon my belly
and not lash out at the simple sky

AFTER TED BERRIGAN

My monkey self
is bigger than
your monkey self!
So help me, God.

LOVELESS

The sky, when it
smells like spermicide,
I grab my coat
and find a place to sit.

ROUGH TRADE

after Peter Schjeldahl

The emerging poet
asserts a wit
embodied in riots
and startling fate.

EPIPHANY

The phone
is on
my wall.

The cat
is on
my lap.

These poems
are not
in French.

CUSTODIAN

Mostly I'm impressed with
the way he avoids
the sound of broken
up prose by limiting
the use of candles
in his apartment complex.

RESOLVE

An old scarecrow
in this valley
of the middle
fingers I have
one and only
one ambulance
to catch up with.

MAN-CHILD

I have a pain not unlike
the many
levels of this poem
with its sticks and its stones
and its physical spell
of broken bones

LOVELESS

Going around my place
shutting windows with my
teeth is the only
eroticism I have left.

PULP

The blue marine
on his knees
in the dark
throat of church.

STRIKE

for Jack Spicer

The match knows the flame's
nothing
        but a one night stand
it can't not have.

DAD

I am running through the fields
with your gun, smiles
in the sun, but
I will not shoot the squirrel.

MOVING

The thought
of leaving
my hometown
when I
don't even
have one.

NIGHT

Each time we enter its dark, open mouth,
we keep ourselves from sliding down
its invisible throat, and we have no idea.
Eventually, its lips close around us,
taking us in, a kiss that knows no end.

THE PULLEY—OR, THIRTEEN WAYS TO ROCK-N-ROLL WITH A BLACKBIRD

1 · THE PULLEY

The river is moving.
The blackbird must be flying.

2

I was of three minds
Like a tree, like a tree, like a tree
I was of three minds
Like, "There's three blackbirds in that tree!"

3

I know no English accents,
Call me stupid and incapable.
But I do know some rhythms,
Yes, I know rhythms, too.
Because the blackbird is involved
In everything I do.

4

A man and a woman
is five words long.
A man and a woman and a blackbird
—three more than that.

5

It was evening all afternoon.
It was snowing
As it was supposed to do.
The blackbird hung
From the cedar limbs
By crazy glue.

6

Icicles filled the long window
With barbaric glass (yeah)
The shadow of the blackbird
Crossed it to and fro (yeah)
The mood traced in the shadow
A cause I can never know (yeah)

7 · A BALLAD

The black
bird whirled
in part
of the pantomime.
It looked
so small
as it shit
into the wind.

8

Aaw tin men of Haddam,
What the hell do you imagine?
Birds of gold! Birds of gold!
Aaw tin men of Haddam,
See 'round the feet o' your women:
Bird of black! Bird of black!

9

I'm torn and I'm tormented,
Please tell me which I prefer:
The blackbird of my sneezes
Or the blackbird of "God bless you."

10

When the blackbird flew (out of sight)
It marked the edge (out of sight)
O the circle of life is—out—of—sight!
         (yeah)

11

He rode over Connecticut.
In a glass coach.
Once a fear pierced him.
In that he mistook.
The shadow he's equipped with.
As a blackbird, baby.
As a blackbird, baby.
As a blackbird, baby, baby, baby, baby.

12

Among twenty snowy buildings
The only thing moving
Was the beak of a blackbird
Working over a plastic straw.

13

At the sight of blackbirds
Flying in a green light,
The poets of tomorrow roll
Like Beethoven in his hole.

HISTORY

after Bill Knott

The period is nothing
but a stoic comma.

CAPITAL

We wander the milky caverns
incompletely aware of the kinds
of treasures we are looking for,
when this ocher-fingered ogre
collars and drags us to its lair,
where it binds us, hand to foot,
and turns us over its fickle fire.

MEMORANDUM

The passenger pigeon
is still extinct.

A READING PUBLIC

A book in the mind
is worth two in the hand
when I rub my eyes
the President decides
to drop some bombs
if any will let him.

DEATH

that constant rider.

CONFESSIONAL

The strong cursive
of the dance
of his adolescence

in living rooms
dark parking lots
and dead ends

in the courtyard
of his own
private
        Osiris.

LOVELESS

It's a solemn man who sits
in socks and underwear
staring through the blinds
waiting for something dear.

RIMBAUD CONSIDERS THE FUTURE

My heart is a toy lost
like a paper sailboat launched
on the swan lake of a John
Ashbery poem—

POEM

Inside the piece of paper
My hand unwinds a watch
The windows tense as drums
I write only about myself.

EVENTRILOQUIST

Poetry does make something happen.
Call it a silent event, acknowledging
its correspondence to the silent e.
But it does not happen on the page
or in the sound waves in the air.
No, what poetry makes happen,
when it's all-over-the-place true,
happens in the lights-out theater of you.

SLEEP

The faceless wraith that ferries us across the lake
and lands us on the foggy shore
where we have been or will have been before.

EDGAR

Lazy thousand spiders in
my Gothic basement home,
I know you're looking out
for Robert Frost.

NATIVE PIECE

Sometimes I feel I am no part in the world,
and it burns because it is a cold wind
and there is no being borne across the skies
the way the skies are broken and borne across time.

POEM

Not everything is
funny the way
looking at yourself
in doorknobs is.

LOVELESS

I tried to chase after you
across the fields, over
the chain-link fence,
but I couldn't hop the fence.

GRAIN

A pint of America
is more than drunk.

NOW

The way I feel you must feel it too,
the gun in a world with no hands.

RETROFUTURISM

The triangle goes *Poof!*
The square goes *Blah!*
The rectangle goes *Moo!*
The circle goes *Ta-da!*

TRANSFORMATIVE LIMITATION

Language is a wall
or a spider on
a wall or a
spider on two walls
or a spider on
two walls and a
ceiling at the same
time I'm writing this.

SCINTILLA

Voice is spark
The one miracle in the night
The noise of light
Opening out
The tongue keeping dark

MORNING

A cape in the wind,
the night begins
to lift. I like you
asleep in the next room,
wrapped in our sheets,
nowhere to be.

POPULISM, CRITICISM, ART

People can sit around and say "I hate poetry." People can sit around and say "Trite and meaningless." But people cannot sit around and say "Hands bum."

SOME LONESOME

poems after Santōka

sitting
passing gas
only the grass can hear

*

chirping sparrow
"what does it take
to be lonesome?"

*

cherry blossoms
bloom and fall
people dance and

*

the woodpecker puts
his ideas into things
what do i do?

*

green leaves
cough and spit
rainwater in my hair

⋆

my friend the mailman
skips my house
again

⋆

bright moon
catching popcorn
in my mouth

⋆

clouds fill the sky
the bombings
are elsewhere

⋆

sun or moon
taking a bath
who cares

⋆

"my way
or the highway"
laughing hard now

★

leaf after leaf
after leaf after
leaf after leaf after

★

shadow
against the wall,
whose deal?

★

hard little marigold
hand on my jeans
i got your third line right here

AUTUMN

The dead leaf is a kind of ghost.
The wind that blows it over,
a kind of booze. How I have loved
you, sleep without dreams.

SIGHT

Another deer
dragged
into the high
roadside grass?

No, just toppled
sawhorses
and sandbags
near

the sun
reflecting on the back
of a construction
sign.

AFFECTIONATE

I can't sleep. Shadows
crawling the walls,
it's almost yesterday—
I need you to hold me.

RAIN (AFTER CREELEY)

Love, if you
love me, spew
your harmless
over me.

QUERY

Why would anyone want to be a poet?
I could be outside, April cool and crisp
as a rear spoiler glazed with frost.
I could get in, start the car, and go
anywhere, or at least to Stop & Shop
to pick up the milk and eggs we need.

A STOP & SHOP IN CONNECTICUT

O cover girl
who has
undone

all
but, oops,
one blouse button,

wouldn't it be
funny if
you

looked
more like
a real woman?

You could be
the shy
cashier;

I
could say,
"Keep the change."

FAITH

after a cartoon by Zachary Kanin

Before the deep, dark wood,
the plump old fairy stood:
"O.K., let's try this again,"
she said, and pointed her wand
at Cinderella's pumpkin head.

MORNING

after Sappho

Moon low and the Pleiades gone,
I remember the midnight
when you were here
as I lie, quarter to the sun, alone.

PAIN SONG, A CENTO

What about the light that comes in
Like a rock or some other heavy thing
The body pushes
If there is any relief from it any slippage
I won't be needing my hat anymore

GOOD GOD

for Tom Hibbard

That blue-jeaned greybeard
was at it again last night,
trying to pluck
the moon from the sky
with his rusty tweezers
so he can sell it back to us
on eBay.

FLING

Love, if you please,
don't dance with me.
My heart's in the trees
where you flung it.

IN TIME, DEAR

You close your eyes
and I am there
sitting on our sofa
with my feet in the ocean
wondering where
you are.

TO AND FRO

Nothing in the birch trees
Nothing in my arms
Nothing in the playground
O, _____, nothing aims to please

FIXING THE RECEPTION

The TV with a condom on it,
stretched over it, so that
I can see the expression
on my face before conception.

IF WE COULD TAKE THE LONG, LONG VIEW, PATRIARCHY MIGHT BE SEEN AS EPHEMERAL, OR AT LEAST WE CAN HOPE

The idea of virginity is involuntary
but we need not flambé our maiden daughters
while manners exist to be prostituted
in the sense that they play out a semi-secret knowledge
the way that Mother was important
as a literary magazine in the 1960s.

PAPER CUTS

for Courtney Love

As a crumpled piece of paper
the world blossoms
sorrows / dawn baskets
what dawn severs
from the inescapable sky.

AN ESCAMOTEUR OF AESTHETICS

Tabletalk. Crosswalk.
Pick my nose for flowers.

⋆

I play the sugar drums and relegate
the sweet mistakes of the sun.
I am breathing and I am wearing
blue jeans and a white T-shirt.

⋆

A body without time—
it makes the brain sway
like a turtleful
of gunpowder and hot air.

⋆

The myth of the right poetics
is almost as bad as
the myth of no poetics at all.

⋆

Big tree.
Big cloud.
Big rock.
Big gun.

*

Mainly my cup of coffee
is a landscape. Little bubble,
the drunken farmboy's hat.

*

It's raining cats and dogs.
It's raining cats and dogs.
It's raining cats and dogs.
It's raining cats and dogs.

*

Well then, you
may never know
the temptation.

*

What is sophistication?
Insufficient innocence.
And insufficient funds?

*

No snowman's-head moon.
No yellow-marker sun.

No bread-crumb star.
No toilet-tree earth.
You are the center of me,
my nothing incarnate.

★

Dirty dishes in the sink.
Poem that goes nowhere.
Life that holds beauty
only because it will end.

THE SUN AFTER KEROUAC

I've come to call you nothing,
O egg fried over hard.

AN ELEGY FOR GINSBERG

People take turns on the couch.
Their minds are OK. Better
than their drugs. I don't know.
Do you? My hands are in
my pockets and my thoughts
are not salacious. Forgive me.

SUNDAY MORNING

The universe is one
vast cenotaph, but
the womb is highly
abstract, a two-word
poem like
          Clockin' wood.

PRAXIS

The thought is enough
to
and sometimes
it's not even close.

ANOTHER PIECE

for Robert Creeley

The emptiness
outside is vast
but not so vast
as the empty
nest inside me.

JOE MO

Dawn percolating
and me
just whizzing
by.

OPPEN ENDED

It is difficult now to speak of
   poetry—
it is that light,
It is the air of atrocity.

GAME

Tomorrow we went to the ballgame
Like it's all been done before
So what, even if, we can steal the blues
Again!

CRINGE

for Ron Silliman

It's the age of huts
all over again
now that the sack
has surpassed the strike.

BIO NOTE

I was born on a day like today
but even more like yesterday.
You want specifics? Well
yesterday's always the same.

SIC

There's something
about living
in the moment
that defies me.

ADVICE

Sand and pyramids
are the essential ingredients of
good plagiarism. It takes
a lot of time and many others.

SPEECH

after Shakespeare

No tongue which does not move in the world.

SING! SING!

"Heaven is a torn and sullied rag
Just like my dad
Have you got the time to find out
Who I really am?"

GUEST

A destination is not a threshold
unless it is.   "I know."
   Let me tell you one more thing.
"The ends of things are splayed
and twinkle?"   Yes.

BODHISATTVA BLUES

What do you remember?
"Walking through the riot.
Making love
like removing bandages.
The end.
But it goes on."

OPENING

> *after Mitch Highfill*

In the summer
she has curated
over our heads
a star chamber
of erotic gears
and sated pens.

SONG

As a dance archives
the feeling of a night,
a song cuts
feeling into time.

FRANK SINATRA

was funny when
he got all mad
and started yelling
and throwing swings.

I miss ol' black
and blue eyes,
the best uncle
I never had

next to Frank like
the blossoms O'Hara.
One was money,
the other freedom.

SMALL TALK

for Kreg Wallace

Sometimes it's hard to tell
if the rain is coming
or going, if the poets
one most enjoys reading
are shivering or just plain old
breathing.

GRIT

That Bukowski
was one tough
shit.

AMERICAN SEASONALS

1

Head out the window
at fifty miles an hour
on the back roads, eyes
closed as the mist
washes my face
with its soft metal cloth.

2

Starry night blossoms
like the bullshit lines
the boys spout
in the parking lot
where I jot this down
in my mother's car.

3

Night arrives like a second
or third chance. I put
my feet up on the ottoman
when my love comes home
with her sonogram
like an Indian summer.

4

What upsets and has you
chucking books and magazines
out the window at
the wind which drives the red leaves down—
there were people all around
and then there were not.

5

A red delicious
twice its size
on the white table
under the window
stuffed with clouds
and falling snow.

GARDE DOWN

I am sick of poetry in books,
in music, in painting, in ballparks.
I want poetry to be the tantrum I throw
because I can't walk on water
or hook up my computer.

HELPLESS

Hoping to feel what is
the empty space
happening between us
whenever the face
of things erases a given
memory, sensation

RIDDLE

Forget the falling fruit, the frost.
Forget whatever you think you know.
Shadowless I creep along,
A summer moss, all green and gold.

PETTY LAMENT

Alright, if I have to be famous, let me be famous
for pilfering the best obscure lines of other poets
and mashing them into incomprehensible art,
or let it be known that, in failing to woo the first girl
I loved, I wept an oasis, and that oasis, when it is
finally discovered, will become the palliative place
where so many lovers will come to end their lives.

UNTITLED (WHITE AND BLACK)

after Mark Rothko

a dozen blank

returns the space

for the poem

DEATH

Leaning forward
to wipe my ass,

I feel my dick
touch the toilet—

it will be like
this, only worse.

COLLISION

When I die
Will you marry me?

AN EVENING

Splintery sun
watering mums,
swat mosquitoes
with a soft hand.

ECHO

"Yea, though I walk
through the Valley of
the Shadow of Death, I
Shall fear no evil—
for I am a lot more
insane than
This Valley."

FINALE

And yet the morning was the piece
of glass on the front of the range
white as the lilacs were last night,
and us inside, a couple of cakes
baking in the dark, hungry for
the light and the cool lemon glaze.

THE WEATHERMAN

I am not
the weather
reports.

SCOTT KEENEY is the author of *Early Returns, Walloping Shrug*, and *Sappho Does Hay(na)ku*. His works have appeared in *Columbia Poetry Review, Mudlark, New York Quarterly, Poetry East*, and other journals. He lives with his family in Connecticut.

www.ingramcontent.com/pod-product-compliance
Lightning Source LLC
Chambersburg PA
CBHW051346040426
42453CB00007B/438